NATIONAL
GEOGRAPHIC

Go for the Gold

PIONEER EDITION

By Ruth Kassinger and Shirleyann Costigan

CONTENTS

Gold
fev

THIERRY OLLIVIER/MUSÉE GUIMET (GETTY IMAGES [HANGING ORNAMENTS]; © SUPER STOCK/AGE FOTOSTOCK (DAGGER); © KEVIN SCHAFER/ALAMY (MASK); © IMAGEBROKER/ALAMY (PENDANT); © PETER HORREE/ALAMY (KNIFE)

er

BY
RUTH KASSINGER

Gold. People moved mountains to find it. Armies invaded countries to control it. Find out how this glittering metal has shaped history.

3

Bill Adair was 19 when he opened the dusty box. He looked at the gold foil inside. One touch, and he caught gold fever. It changed him forever. Gold became his life's work.

Born in Earth

Gold is the metal that changed Adair's life. It formed deep in Earth long ago. Scientists think volcanoes heated underground water. The hot water melted the gold. Liquid gold then flowed with the water into cracks between rocks. The shiny metal cooled and hardened, forming **veins** of gold. In some places, they reached near Earth's surface.

Rivers streamed over the rocky surface, wearing it away. Over time, the gold showed through. Gold nuggets broke loose. They sat in the stream, until they were discovered.

The Egyptians caught gold fever about 5,000 years ago. Since then, gold has been found in many places. Each time, the fever grows. Let's look at some golden times in history.

Old Money. *This gold coin is more than 2,000 years old.*

The Fever Spreads

Egypt, 3,000 B.C.E. The pharaohs, or kings of Egypt, loved gold. They wore golden crowns and jewelry. They ruled from golden thrones. Their mummies wore masks of gold. Soon, gold became harder to find.

The pharaohs captured slaves to mine gold for them. Deep in Earth, the miners cracked rocks with fire. Poisonous gas filled the air. Miners lay on their backs under falling rocks. The rocks often crushed them. Many slaves died mining gold.

Egypt traded gold for things from other countries. **Trade routes** stretched from Egypt to China. When people traveled the trade routes, they spread gold fever.

Gold Coins

Turkey, 560 B.C.E. King Croesus ruled ancient Lydia, now in Turkey. He had the idea to **mint,** or make, coins. Gold was a great metal to use. It lasts a long time. It's rare, so it's worth a lot. It is soft enough to form into shapes.

People made gold coins that were the same size, weight, and value. This made buying and selling things easier. The idea of gold coins spread around the world, bringing gold fever with it.

Ancient Art. *Bill Adair caught gold fever when he was a teenager. Now he puts gold leaf on picture frames.*

Famous Face. *This gold mask was found on King Tut's mummy.*

Crowning Touch. *This crown belonged to a princess. She could fold it flat when she traveled.*

Gold in the Americas

South America, 1500s In the 1500s, word of a **ceremony** spread across Europe. *In South America, a king stands on a raft. He is covered in gold dust. He drops piles of gold into the lake to please his god.*

People asked: Did the golden king have a golden city? The story grew. People named the city El Dorado.

Spanish explorers went to South America to search for the city. They never found it. Yet they did find gold. They killed many people to get it.

The Sun King was an Inca leader. In 1532, a Spanish gold hunter found the king's city. His soldiers shot 2,000 men and captured the Sun King. The gold hunter promised to free the king for a roomful of gold. He got his gold but killed the king anyway. Some people would do anything for gold.

California, 1848 In 1848, a man found gold in California. The news spread. Thousands of Americans dropped everything and went west to search for gold. It wasn't easy. Many got sick. Some found gold. Others did not. But the gold hunters kept coming.

Gold's Global Grip

Worldwide, 2009 Today, finding gold is harder than ever. Miners sometimes have to dig thirty tons of rock just to find enough gold for one ring! That leaves huge holes in the ground. To get gold from rocks, many miners use a poisonous metal called mercury. It can make people sick. It can also harm the environment.

Even so, people use more gold than ever before. Today, it is used for more than jewelry. It is used in computers and cell phones. Astronauts wear **visors** coated with gold. It protects them from the sun's rays. Someday, gold might even fight cancer.

Thousands of years separate the pharaohs from today's scientists, and artists, like Bill Adair. Yet one thing unites them all: gold fever.

wordwise

ceremony: special actions and words used to celebrate an important event

mint: to make, or manufacture, coins

trade route: path that people traveled to sell and buy goods

vein: narrow layer of mineral that forms in the crack of a rock

visor: shield on the front of a helmet that protects the face

© BOLTIN PICTURE LIBRARY/THE BRIDGEMAN ART LIBRARY

Buried Treasure. *These golden arms were found in Peru. Today, much of the world's gold comes from Peru.*

© DECO/ALAMY

Golden God. *The Inca called gold "the sweat of the sun." They used gold to make this sun god.*

© PAM RANCIS/PHOTOGRAPHER'S CHOICE/GETTY IMAGES

Sun Shield. *This is a model of an astronaut's helmet. A thin layer of gold protects the astronaut from the sun's rays.*

Made with GOLD

© STEFFEN FOERSTER/SHUTTERSTOCK.COM

It sparkles. It glows. But why is gold really so valuable? For one, it is strong, and lasts a long time. Gold is also easily shaped. And gold is rare. In all history, only 161,000 tons of gold have been mined. That's enough to fit into just two large swimming pools. No wonder people find it so special!

Here are some of the many things that are made with gold.

EYE OF SCIENCE/PHOTO RESEACHERS, INC.

ELECTRONICS

Gold transfers heat and electricity well. So people often use it in electronic devices and computers. The gold wires inside many circuit boards are about the size of a human hair.

AFOTO6267/SHUTTERSTOCK.COM

JEWELRY

Is jewelry ever made of "pure gold"? It can be, but it might get scratched. Today, most jewelers mix gold with other metals. That way gold rings and necklaces stay scratch-free.

SPACE TECHNOLOGY

Gold does not break down easily. That's one reason it is valuable for use in spacecrafts. Nearly 41 kilograms (90 pounds) of gold were used in the U.S. Columbia space shuttle, shown here.

COLUMBIA SPACE SHUTTLE/NASA

© BEN EDWARDS/GETTY IMAGES

DENTISTRY

People have used gold in teeth for thousands of years. Here, a gold crown is being fitted onto a model. Later, it will be attached to a real tooth.

HOW GOLD IS USED
(in tons for 2008)

BUYING & SELLING GOLD TO MAKE MONEY (1183.4)

DENTISTRY (55.9)

OTHER INDUSTRIAL USES (86.9)

ELECTRONICS (292.7)

JEWELRY (2186.7)

© ISTOCKPHOTO.COM

Source: World Gold Council

Desert T

By Shirleyann Costigan

Past and Present. *A twenty-mule team hauls borax out of Death Valley (top). The moon rises over the colorful rocks of Zabriskie Point (bottom).*

Treasure

In the past, pioneers came to Death Valley, California, in search of gold. Now people are beginning to see a different kind of treasure here. It's all around them!

Death Valley's name fits it well. The valley is the hottest, driest spot in North America. The valley is part of a larger desert called the Mojave (moh HAH vee).

Very little rain falls each year. Some years there is no rain at all. Temperatures may rise above 49° Celsius (120° Fahrenheit). Yet people have lived here for thousands of years. Let's learn their stories.

At Home in the Heat

Death Valley was not always a desert. It was once a lake. When people first arrived, it was still a lake. That was about 10,000 years ago. About 1,000 years ago, the ancestors of today's Timbisha people came to the valley.

Over time, the valley changed. It got hotter. Less rain fell. The lake dried up. Still, the Timbisha stayed. They learned how to live in the desert.

The Timbisha hunted desert animals and harvested plants for food. They moved near freshwater springs. They built homes from desert shrubs.

In the hottest months, they moved into the cooler mountains. They lived this life for centuries. Then, in 1849, **pioneers** came from the East.

The Lost Pioneers

The first pioneers to travel across Death Valley were lost. They were trying to find a shorter way to the California gold fields.

Their wagons were breaking. They were starving. They were thirsty. Then, on Christmas Eve, they found water in Timbisha territory.

The pioneers rested and talked about what to do. "We all felt pretty much downhearted," one of the men wrote. "Our provisions were getting so scarce that all must be saved for the women and children. The men must get along on ox meat alone."

View of the Valley

Long Walk

The pioneers split into groups. Each group had its own plan. One group headed toward the far mountains.

The journey grew harder. The oxen had little to eat. They became too weak to pull the wagons. The pioneers had to leave their wagons behind. They killed the oxen for food. Luckily, it was winter. They could drink water from melted snow and ice.

Finally, the pioneers crossed over the mountains and out of the desert. The tough trip did not scare other people away. New pioneers followed. They, too, were searching for gold.

Four-Legged Food. *Native Americans hunted bighorn sheep and painted them on rocks.*

Thirsty Valley. *From Zabriskie Point, you can see the tough landscape that people have faced in Death Valley.*

The Fortune Hunters

Valuable **ores** lay hidden under Death Valley. Fields of gold and silver were scattered around the area. Early California miners came for the gold. Many of them settled in Death Valley.

First came the **prospectors.** They searched for the gold fields. When they made a **strike,** the word got out: *Gold! Gold!* Miners rushed to the area. They set up mining camps. The camps grew into towns. The towns grew into cities.

During the late 1800s and early 1900s, mining towns sprouted up everywhere. But when the gold mines dried up, the miners left. The cities died and became ghost towns.

Twenty-Mule Teams

Miners came for more than gold. Some came to mine a kind of salt that was made into borax. Borax was used to make glass and cleaning products.

In the 1880s, William T. Coleman had a borax factory in Death Valley. He used twenty-mule teams to carry huge loads of borax to the railroads. Each team pulled two full wagons, plus a water tank, across the desert.

Tough Job

The route ran 265 kilometers (165 miles) out of Death Valley. The journey was hard. It took courage. One bad step, and the mule team could run the wagons off a cliff.

The driver cracked a whip to get the mules' attention. But mostly, he used just his voice to guide them. When the driver spoke, the mules knew he wasn't fooling and obeyed.

Death Valley Today

Today, Death Valley is a national park. Tourists come to see natural sites such as Badwater Basin and the sandy Eureka Dunes. They also come to see the colored clay at Artists Palette.

The mining days of Death Valley are long gone. Ghost towns are all that remain. Through it all, the Timbisha stayed. This valley is still their home. For them, it is a valley of life.

A Gift for Gold. *Shorty Harris, pictured at right, was Death Valley's most famous gold hunter. He made a big strike in 1904.*

Prized Park. *Death Valley once lured miners. Today, it draws nearly a million tourists every year.*

Wordwise

ore: substance mined for its value

pioneer: one of the first people to move to a new place

prospector: person who searches a place for gold or other valuable material

strike: discovery of something valuable

The Search for Gold

It's time to dig into what you learned about the search for gold.

1 Where does gold come from?

2 Picture the ceremony of the golden king. What did he look like? What did he do?

3 How did "gold fever" change the history of Death Valley?

4 What treasures can you find in Death Valley today?

5 Why do you think people care so much about gold?

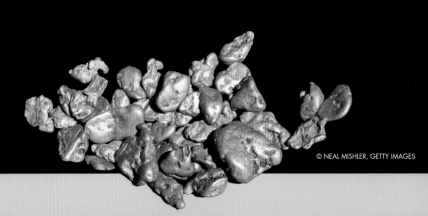